Today's Superst☆rs
Entertainment

Will Smith

by Susan K. Mitchell

GARETH**STEVENS**
GS
P U B L I S H I N G
A Member of the WRC Media Family of Companies

Please visit our web site at: www.garethstevens.com
For a free color catalog describing Gareth Stevens Publishing's
list of high-quality books and multimedia programs, call
1-800-542-2595 (USA) or 1-800-387-3178 (Canada).
Gareth Stevens Publishing's fax: (414) 332-3567.

Library of Congress Cataloging-in-Publication Data

Mitchell, Susan K.
    Will Smith / by Susan K. Mitchell.
       p. cm. — (Today's superstars. Entertainment)
    Includes bibliographical references and index.
    ISBN-13: 978-0-8368-7653-6 (lib. bdg.)
    1. Smith, Will, 1968- —Juvenile literature. 2. Actors—United States—
Biography—Juvenile literature. 3. Rap musicians—United States—Biography—
Juvenile literature. I. Title.
PN2287.W612M58   2007
791.4302'8092—dc22
   [B]   2006031219

This edition first published in 2007 by
Gareth Stevens Publishing
A Member of the WRC Media Family of Companies
330 West Olive Street, Suite 100
Milwaukee, WI 53212 USA

Editor: Gini Holland
Art direction and design: Tammy West
Picture research: Sabrina Crewe

Photo credits: cover, pp. 17, 22, 27, 28 Associated Press; p. 5 © 20th Century
Fox/courtesy Everett Collection; pp. 7, 21 © Columbia Pictures/courtesy Everett
Collection; p. 8 © Chris Pizzello/Reuters/Corbis; p. 11 © Stephane Cardinale/
People Avenue/Corbis; p. 13 © David Bergmann/Corbis; pp. 16, 18 © Neal
Preston/Corbis; p. 20 © Lisa O'Connor/ZUMA/Corbis; p. 25 © Warner Brothers/
courtesy Everett Collection

Printed in the United States of America

1 2 3 4 5 6 7 8 9 10 10 09 08 07 06

Contents

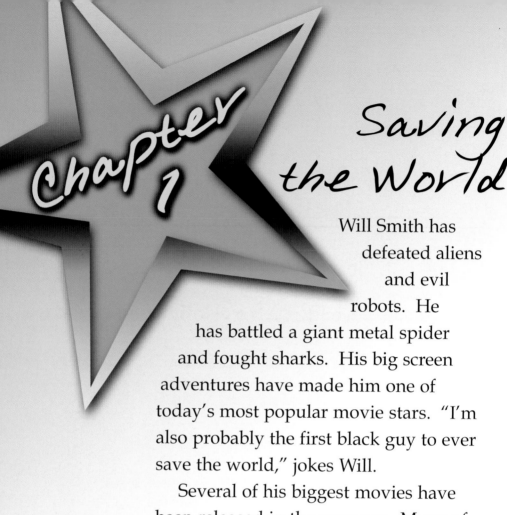

Chapter 1

Saving the World

Will Smith has defeated aliens and evil robots. He has battled a giant metal spider and fought sharks. His big screen adventures have made him one of today's most popular movie stars. "I'm also probably the first black guy to ever save the world," jokes Will.

Several of his biggest movies have been released in the summer. Many of them released on July Fourth weekend. "That's my weekend — July Fourth. I own that," says Will. With the success of movies such as *Independence Day* and *Men In Black*, Will has become the king of the summer blockbuster.

Total Will Appeal
Part of Will Smith's charm is the way he can relate to many different people. Will

grew up in an African American and Jewish neighborhood. He went to a mostly white elementary school. His high school was mainly African American. Will went to a Baptist church and often hung out with Muslim friends. He learned to connect with all kinds of people, which later helped him in his work. "I'm able to find the joke that everyone thinks is hilarious, the record everyone thinks is moving," he said.

Will trained with real Marine pilots for his role in the 1996 movie *Independence Day*.

CAPT. STEVEN HILLER
"EAGLE"

Will has charmed not only movie audiences, but other actors, too. He has starred with several Oscar winners. Many actors like to work with Will because of his fun attitude. "Will is double cool," says *Men In Black* costar Tommy Lee Jones.

Big Willie's Style

Most stars are famous for doing one thing very well. For example, some act, some sing, some rap, and some dance. A few stars become famous for more than one talent. They might start with acting, and then cross over to something else, such as singing, and get famous for that, too. They are called cross-over artists. Will is one of the most famous cross-over artists in history.

He has achieved success as a rap artist. He crossed over to TV and had a hit show. Then Will made his name in movies.

Anything Will has put his mind to, he has accomplished. Few people can claim success in this many areas of entertainment.

Fact File

Men In Black was based on a little-known comic book by Lowell Cunningham.

Summer Movie Magic

What is a blockbuster? A blockbuster is a movie that makes a lot of money. Most blockbusters earn more than one hundred million dollars in the United States. The first summer blockbuster was *Jaws* in 1975. It made more than four hundred million dollars worldwide. Since then, summer has become the main money-making season for Hollywood.

The slime in the 1997 movie *Men In Black* was actually edible. Will called it "terribly disgusting."

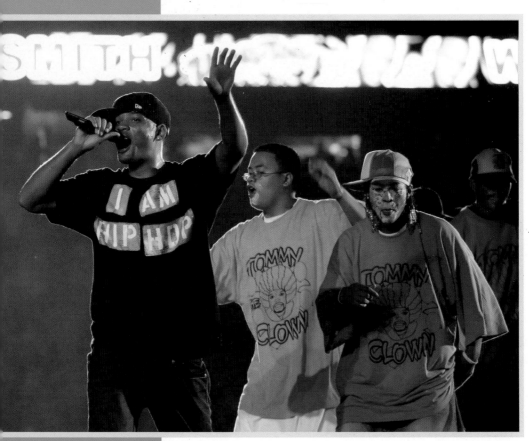

Will Smith (*left*) performs at the Wango Tango 2005 concert at Angel Stadium in Anaheim, California. Will is not the only one in his family who performs at concerts. His wife, Jada Pinkett-Smith, has her own band called Wicked Wisdom.

He has earned many awards for his work both in music and acting. He has been listed in *Ebony* magazine's Top 40 earners' list. He has been listed as one of the most powerful celebrities by *Forbes* magazine. In 2006, *Time* magazine named him one of the 100 Most Influential People. "When you enjoy what you do, you're gonna get good at it," says Will.

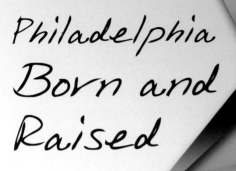

Philadelphia Born and Raised

Chapter 2

Willard Christopher Smith Jr. was born on September 25, 1968, in Philadelphia, Pennsylvania. His parents, Willard Sr. and Caroline, both worked full-time. Will's mother worked as an administrator for the local Board of Education. His father owned his own refrigeration business. Will has an older sister named Pamela and younger siblings, twins Harry and Ellen.

Will's family lived in the middle class neighborhood of Wynnefield. School and discipline were always important to Will's parents. His mother made sure Will got good grades. His father, a former drill sergeant, believed in following the rules. He made sure Will worked hard and stayed out of trouble.

Crowned Prince

As a boy, Will went to a private Catholic school. He was a good student who did well in math and science. Will loved attention and was often the class clown. His personality earned him the nickname Prince Charming from his teachers.

Will was also a clown at home. His grandmother, Helen Bright, saw that Will was a natural performer. She often gave him parts in the church plays she put together for the community.

Another big influence in the Smith house was music. Everyone in Will's family played an instrument. His father played guitar, and Will took piano lessons. "There were instruments around the house, and I just played a little bit of everything," said Will. He got his first stereo when he was ten years old.

Will loved to listen to music by funk bands.

When Will was thirteen, his parents divorced. He continued to live with

Fact File

Will liked dinosaurs as a young student and could name them all. Stegosaurus was his favorite.

One Brick at a Time

Will's father was loving but tough. When Will was twelve, his father made Will and his brother fix a brick wall in their yard. They had to mix concrete and lay the bricks one at a time. Will thought they would never be able to do it. The wall took six months to finish. The day it was finished, Will's father told him, "Don't you ever tell me there's something that you can't do."

"The only people I ever idolized are my parents," said Will. His mother joins him here at the thirtieth Cesar Awards Ceremony held at the Chatelet in Paris, in 2005.

his mother. Will's father still played a big role in raising his kids. It was also about this time that Will discovered rap music.

School of Rap

Soon, Will was earning money and becoming known as a top rapper at parties. He hit the streets to win local rap contests. His grades began to slide and Will's parents were concerned. One day, Will's father drove him through some of the worst streets in Philadelphia. Will saw people lying in doorways and some on drugs. He saw what failing in school could lead to. He promised his parents he would put more effort into school work.

Will worked hard and brought his grades back up. He began rapping with a local DJ named Jeff Townes after meeting him at a party in 1984. Jeff Townes was already known as DJ Jazzy Jeff. Will needed a name to go with his rap persona. He thought back to his school nickname, Prince Charming. He made a few changes and the Fresh Prince was born.

Fact File

The 1979 hit "Rapper's Delight" by the Sugar Hill Gang got Will into rapping. He also thought Dr. Seuss stories sounded a lot like rap.

Roots of Rap

Rap is kind of storytelling set to a beat. It often rhymes, like poetry. Rap has roots in Jamaican and African music. It came out of African American "street" music in the United States. In the early '80s, groups like Run DMC helped rap become more popular. Some rap artists use lyrics about violence and crime in their music. Will never did.

Will Smith often performs to raise money for charity. On July 2, 2005, he performed at the *Live 8* concert in front of the Philadelphia Museum of Art.

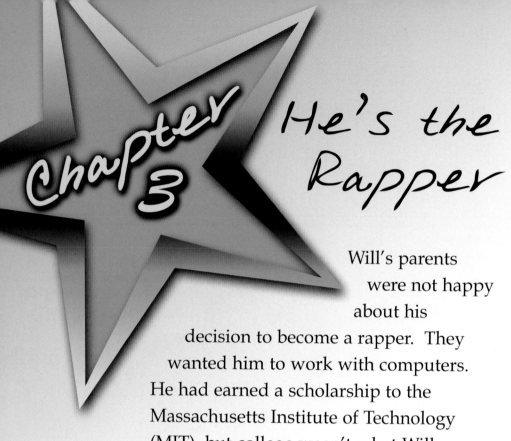

Chapter 3

He's the Rapper

Will's parents were not happy about his decision to become a rapper. They wanted him to work with computers. He had earned a scholarship to the Massachusetts Institute of Technology (MIT), but college wasn't what Will wanted. Will was sure he and Jeff could make it big. Will's parents agreed to give him a year. He promised that if he didn't make it in rap, he would go to college. It wasn't a promise he would have to keep.

By 1987, Will had his first hit song, "Girls Ain't Nothing But Trouble." He and Jeff were on their way. They had a fun style of party rap. They rapped about typical teenage experiences, such as dating and parents. Their popular humor and clean rap lyrics helped shoot them to the top of the charts.

Their first album, *Rock the House*, began to win awards. Soon, friends and money were in big supply. Will started spending more than he was making. He had a mansion, six cars, and two motorcycles. His parents were worried about him. Will's father asked him, "What do you need six cars for if you only have one butt?"

Losing It All

By the end of 1989, Will was broke. He owed millions of dollars in taxes. He sold everything and moved back in with his mother. Will's third album was not selling well, either. He needed a change and decided to try acting.

Will got lucky during the taping of a popular talk show. Quincy Jones was a guest. Will was invited backstage, where he met Mr. Jones and a music executive named Benny Medina.

Mr. Medina wanted to turn his own life story into a TV show. Mr. Medina had been adopted by a wealthy and loving family as a child. Mr. Medina liked Will. Will

Fact File

Other rappers said Will and Jeff weren't producing "real" rap because of their lighthearted lyrics. Will and Jeff refused to change their style.

Will Smith jumps in the air outside the studio during a break in taping his television comedy, *The Fresh Prince of Bel Air.*

reminded him of himself. He wanted Will in the starring role. Will knew this was a great chance. If he could land this role, he could "cross over" from rapping into acting.

The producers of the show were not sure a rapper could be a good actor. The other actors on the show were worried, too. They had trained for years. Could an untrained actor do the job?

Before he could get the role, Will had to audition for the show. Fortunately, he did very well. He impressed the show's producers. With Quincy Jones's help, he began work on *The Fresh Prince of Bel Air* in 1990. Will knew he was back on track. This time, he felt ready to handle success.

Rocking the Music Awards

In 1989, Will and Jeff's second album, *He's the DJ,*
I'm the Rapper, was nominated for a Grammy award. It
was the first time rap was included as an award category.
Will and Jeff refused to attend because their part of the
award ceremony would not be shown on TV. They felt rap
should be just as important as more popular music. Their
stand made a difference. The next year, the rap category
was televised.

Before the Grammys, Will and Jeff received their first awards at the American Music Awards. In 1989, they won awards for Best Rap Album and Best Rap Artist.

The Power of Q

Quincy Jones is one of the most powerful people in show business. He began his career in the 1950s as a trumpet player for several great jazz musicians. Quincy also became a great composer, writing many original pieces of music. He holds the record for the most Grammy nominations, with more than seventy to his name. In 1964, he became the first African American executive at Mercury Records. He has produced movies such as *The Color Purple*. He works hard to promote African American talent in music, TV, and movies.

Quincy Jones worked to get Will the lead in *The Fresh Prince of Bel Air*. Here, they relax on the set in 1990.

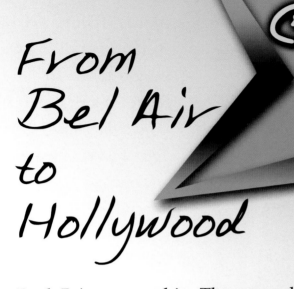

From Bel Air to Hollywood

Fresh Prince was a hit. The same charm Will used on his teachers as a kid worked on TV audiences as well. His acting needed work, but Will held his own with the more experienced cast. Playing the main character, also named "Will," wasn't much of a stretch for the rapper turned actor.

While working on his TV show, Will still made rap albums with DJ Jazzy Jeff. They released several albums, such as *And In This Corner …*, *Homebase*, and *Code Red*. Will and Jeff's music continued to win awards.

As Will's acting got better, he wanted to try something

Fact File

Will was afraid of forgetting his lines. So, he memorized the whole script. In early shows, you can see Will's lips moving as other actors speak!

Will has often been a winner at the *Nickelodeon* Kids' Choice Awards. In 2005, he and his second wife, actress Jada Pinkett-Smith, brought Will's son, Trey, and their children, Jaden and Willow, to the Eighteenth Annual Awards ceremony.

more difficult. So, he began to audition for movie roles. In 1992, he got his first part in *Where the Day Takes You*. His role was a homeless teen in a wheelchair. It was a small one, but Will's acting ability got great reviews. That same year, Will married Sheree Zampino and they had a son named Trey.

Will's next big break came when he won the role of Paul in *Six Degrees of Separation*. It was different from anything he had done before. Movie critics praised him. Will was finally taken seriously as an actor.

Will's life became very busy. He was working on a TV show, making rap albums, and acting in movies. All of this left little time for family. His marriage paid the price. In 1995, Will and Sheree divorced. They agreed to share custody of their son.

Bad Boys, Good Comedy

Also in 1995, Will played his first action hero role in *Bad Boys*. His costar was a comedian named Martin Lawrence. The roles were originally written for white comedians Jon Lovitz and Dana Carvey. The script was not finished when filming began. To fill in, Will and Martin made up many of the lines.

Will worked out hard to put muscle on his lanky frame to play a Miami police detective with Martin Lawrence in *Bad Boys*.

Still Making Music

Will found more success writing songs to go with his movies. No longer the Fresh Prince, he became Big Willie. His name changed, but not his style. He still kept his hip-hop beat and fun lyrics. Songs like "Gettin' Jiggy Wit It," "Men In Black," and "Wild, Wild West" earned Will several music awards as a solo artist. His albums, *Big Willie Style*, in 1997, and *Willennium*, in 1999, both sold several million copies.

Will keeps on rapping. Here, he performs at the 2002 Berlin premier of *Men In Black II*. Even with his solo success, Will still works with Jeff Townes on many of his hit songs.

New Directions

His marriage was not the only thing ending. After six years, Will decided it was time to end *The Fresh Prince of Bel Air*, too. He wanted to stop while he was still on top. During this fast-changing time in his life, Will got the script that would make him a superstar.

Independence Day was a big movie with an all-star cast. It was released on July Fourth weekend in 1996. It was a huge success. Will Smith played Captain Steve Hiller, a wise-cracking pilot who takes on invading aliens. It was the first of many movies where Will saves the world.

The next year, Will costarred with Tommy Lee Jones in *Men In Black*. As in *Independence Day*, Will had to protect Earth from aliens. Both movies earned huge amounts of money at the box office.

Riding high on his film success, Will married actress Jada Pinkett. They had known each other since his TV days and had remained friends. In 1998, their first child, son Jaden, was born. His daughter, Willow, was born in 2000.

Fact File

Jada Pinkett-Smith tried out for the role of Will's girlfriend on *The Fresh Prince of Bel Air*. She was thought to be too short for the part, so she was not hired.

Chapter 5

The Will to Succeed

Will was in demand, but he wanted new challenges. Not wanting to be only an action hero, he took roles which showed his range as an actor. He had his first starring role in 1998 with *Enemy of the State*. It was the first movie where Will didn't have a costar to back him. He also played a mysterious golf caddy in *The Legend of Bagger Vance*. These movies did not earn as much money as his first few films. Will's reputation as an actor, however, continued to grow.

One film was good enough to earn him an Oscar nomination. In 2001, Will starred in *Ali*. The movie was based on the life of famous boxer, Muhammad Ali. It was the first time a rap artist had ever been up for

Win Some, Lose Some

Not all of Will's movies were winners. *Wild, Wild West* was a combination science fiction and old west movie. Although it made good money, critics hated it. It even won a "Razzie" award for Worst Movie. Most critics did agree, however, that Will and costar Kevin Kline did the best they could with a bad movie.

25

an Oscar. Will did not win the award, but being nominated was a huge honor. It showed that both critics and the movie industry respected his acting skills.

His next movies were the sequels *Men In Black II* and *Bad Boys II*. Both did very well at the box office. They also brought Will back together with two of his favorite costars, Tommy Lee Jones and Martin Lawrence. Adding to his streak of "saving the world," Will starred in the thriller *I, Robot* in 2004. In this film, Earth was in danger from robots, not aliens.

Still Ruling

Today, Will continues to push himself as an actor. In 2005, he starred in *Hitch*, his first romantic comedy. He even provided the voice to a fast-talking fish in the animated movie *Shark Tale*. Will continues to be a big box-office draw and is always in demand in Hollywood. He has several movie projects lined up through 2008. He has completed filming

Fact File

In his early career, Will auditioned for the role of Robin in *Batman Forever*. He lost the part to Chris O'Donnell.

"I Am the Greatest"

Muhammad Ali is one of the greatest boxing champs in history. Born Cassius Clay, he began boxing in the late 1950s. He changed his name when he converted to Islam. Ali began boxing when he was twelve and his bike was stolen. The police officer who helped him with his stolen bike was also the local boxing coach. Muhammad Ali is known for his bold personality. He often declared himself to be "the greatest."

Will did not use a stunt double in *Ali*. He learned to box and did all the fight scenes himself. With his son Trey at his side, he squares off with the great fighter himself at the premiere of *Ali* in 2001.

Will struts his stuff as a rapper on *The Today Show* Summer Concert Series in 2005.

The Pursuit of Happyness. In this drama, Will stars with his younger son, Jaden. He is also filming another sci-fi film called *I Am Legend.* He continues to produce albums and win awards.

Will is now a dedicated husband and father. The value of hard work that he learned from his parents continues to pay off for him. "You would be surprised how many things will start to happen once you remove the 'I can't' from your sentences," Will says. "I've learned to start my sentences with 'I can do . . .' anything."

Fact File

Will added *author* to his list of job titles in 2001. His picture book, *Just the Two of Us*, was based on a song about his oldest son, Trey.

28

Time Line

1963	Willard Christopher Smith Jr. is born in Philadelphia on September 25.
1987	Releases first album with DJ Jeff, *Rock the House*.
1989	Wins the first Grammy for Best Rap Performance ever given.
1990	Stars in TV show, *The Fresh Prince of Bel Air*.
1993	Appears in *Made in America* and *Six Degrees of Separation*.
1996	Final episode of *The Fresh Prince of Bel Air*. Costars in summer blockbuster, *Independence Day*.
1997	Costars in *Men In Black*.
1998	First starring role in *Enemy of the State*. Wins first solo Grammy.
2001	Stars in *Ali*.
2002	Costars in *Men In Black II*. Nominated for an Oscar for role in *Ali*.
2003	Named one of *Time* magazine's 100 Most Influential People.

Glossary

audition — in acting, a sample performance by an actor given to show his or her ability.

costar — one of two actors who have equal roles in a movie, a play, or a TV show.

critics — in acting, people whose job is to give their opinions about movies or TV shows.

crossover artists — people who have success in many different areas of entertainment. Years ago, it referred to African American artists who appealed to a white audience, or whose appeal crossed over racial lines.

executive — a top person in a company who decides how things will be done.

funk — a combination of jazz, soul, and blues music with heavy rhythm and bass beats.

Grammy — an award given by the Recording Academy, a group of people who work in the music business. It is the highest award a musician can get.

lyrics — words to a song.

Oscar — an award given by the Academy of Motion Picture Arts and Sciences, a group of people who work in the movie business. It is the highest award an actor can get.

persona — someone's public image or personality.

Razzie — an award given by the Golden Raspberry Award Foundation, founded by author John Wilson.

To Find Out More

Books

The History of Rap Music. African American Achievers (series). Cookie Lommel (Chelsea House)

Will Smith. Scene! (series). Dave Stern (Aladdin Paperbacks)

Will Smith. Galaxy of Superstars (series). Meg Green (Chelsea House)

Will Smith. African-American Biography Library (series). Michael A. Schuman (Enslow)

Will Smith. Black Americans of Achievement (series). Stacey Stauffer (Chelsea House)

Videos

Shark Tale (DreamWorks) PG

The Fresh Prince of Bel Air — The Complete First Four Seasons DVD (Warner Home Video) NR

The Will Smith Music Video Collection (Sony) NR

Web Sites

Will Smith
www.willsmith.com
Official Web site. Photo, audio, and video clips, and many extras.

Publishers note to educators and parents: Our editors have carefully reviewed this Web site to ensure that it is suitable for children. Many Web sites change frequently, however, and we cannot guarantee that a site's future contents will continue to meet our high standards of quality and educational value. Be advised that children should be closely supervised whenever they access the Internet.

Index

About the Author

Susan K. Mitchell has always loved books, movies, and music. She has also been a fan of Will Smith since she was a teenager. She is a preschool teacher and author of several children's picture books. Susan has also written numerous magazine articles for both adults and children on many different subjects. She lives near Houston, Texas, with her husband, their German Shepherd, two cats, two fish, and an adopted pet squirrel. She dedicates this book to her parents, Robbie and William Floyd, who always believed in her.